Tommy Sissons is a twenty-year-old is the 2014 SLAMbassadors national in the 2014 Roundhouse Poetry Slam Hammer and Tongue slam champion. He has performed in venues across the UK such as the Royal Albert Hall, the Roundhouse Theatre and the Birmingham Reparatory Theatre, in addition to festivals such as Latitude, Bestival, Camp Bestival and Boomtown. He is also the narrator of Channel 4's award-winning TV series Four to the Floor. Other clients of his include BBC Radio 1, Red Bull, the Imperial War Museum, the National Trust and the Guardian. His poetry has been studied by creative writing and literature students at the University of Trier in Germany and, in addition to this, he has taught spoken word at the V&A Museum and a variety of schools across the country.

Goodnight Son

Tommy Sissions

This edition published by Burning Eye Books 2016

www.burningeye.co.uk
@burningeyebooks

Burning Eye Books
15 West Hill, Portishead, BS20 6LG

ISBN 978-1-909136-84-7

CONTENTS

CHILDREN OF ICARUS

We know sirens better than the voice of our fathers,
Empty houses await guardian angels,
Mothers in supermarkets inform them their children
have gone out for the night
So they will not be back for the week.

Teachers have not seen them,
Headmasters do not recognise them,
Newspapers do not know them yet.

Mathematics and science are used outside the
classroom,
Money is kept in shoeboxes, not bank branches,
New languages are learnt,
Boys believe they return as men.

The skeleton of Icarus lies washed up on a beach,
Children gather round but do not recognise it.
When they tire of it they will leave,
And it will call to them – but they are gone,
'Where were you when your guardian angel came
knocking?'

DEPTFORD MARKET

The fish are all gutted by the pavement.
An old lass with weary eyes
Pushes a knife against them
So they are fresh for you and I.

Hardmanship and juice boxes go hand in hand
For the lads who bop on these roads.
They have been raised on ackee and saltfish, curried
goat and cowfoot,
Vegetarianism is non-existent.

Is that a new tracksuit?
Wear it with materialistic prowess
And show it off to the hungriest amongst the people.
It will make a mockery of the knock-off sportswear
That hangs with the rugs and second-hand shoes.

Your mother sings to herself in Barclays,
A low chant at the cashpoint.
Your idols linger outside the bookie's on the corner
of the estate.
Make eye contact with them but say nothing.

Counting lost teeth – their daily profession.
Guinness punch – their daily lip-wetter.
Their daily adversaries serve to keep the peace
But accomplish less harmony than grief.

The air tastes of candlewax and fish on ice,
The scent of a working week for the locals,
The scent of home for the children with faces like
scrunched-up pieces of paper
And the eyes of old men.

One boy practises imaginary weightlifting with his father,
Waking his tender biceps.
He will move on to tins of beans and then to dumbbells,
And there will be kids at school like bruised bananas.

Mountain bikes are good
But motorbikes are quicker.
People will think you are richer,
Which can be both good and bad.

A tattooed scarecrow walks with her old skinhead prince,
Beside the Bashment boutiques
Where the girls wait around for their bargain price weaves
And dream of divas in celebrity magazines.

There is an old man with a face like a chewed-on dummy.
He is no stranger to the butcher shop carcasses.
He likes his chicken and chips, coco jerk and fried dumplings
As much as the kids in the Nike Swoosh peak caps
Who have shaped their own language
But still understand patois.

ELEGY FOR THE YOUNG

If I were to be slain by the blind youth,
If I were to be slain by the sword of reputation,
Would you write a poem for me?

I write an elegy for the young on the back of the
guns
That we use to prove our adulthood,
I hold an elegy for the young on the back of my
tongue
For every day I will update it.

We are dying,
We are killing each other.

I go to sleep on the thought of dead young men
With News at Ten Trevor McDonald lullabies.
In these last six months alone,
Four lads I'd once known have died.

And if you stand there today and ask me why,
Examine the anguish I have seen with these eyes,
I will reply:

We were raised in a society
Where there seems to be a new drama every single
week
And the same words echo when I hear my friends
speak.
'I need to get away,' they tell me, 'I need to leave,'
But living in the gutter, you will only go as far as the
end of your street.

There is a simple solution

That we are too young and ignorant to see:
Go for your dreams,
Don't let the world hold you down and you can
achieve.

And yet so many of us
Still dedicate our time to meaningless beef.
We were not taught to bury the hatchet but embed it
instead.
Young men can never be taken for a mug,
We would sooner die on our feet
Than live with our reputation in shreds.

And so we go about our lives not giving a fuck,
Fatherless fathers and fatherless sons,
So we stab each other in raves
But when eye contact can get you killed
We have to question what we have really become.

Because it wasn't long ago we blared Crazy Frog
ringtones
And played with water pistols in the streets.
Now we stab shopkeepers during schooltime lunch
breaks
And our neighbours lay down reefs.

They knock years off your life while you sit behind
bars,
When you leave you'll be minus sweet sixteen,
But the demise of our youth is the death of our
future
Or is that not obvious to see?

That's why I'm shocked
When I hear of the Deghayes brothers killed in war-
torn Syria,
That's why I'm confused
When I hear of Ibby Kamara radicalised into jihadist
militia,
When I remember him kicking about a football at
our school
And comparing Busta Rhymes's flow
To that of Orifice Vulgatron from Foreign Beggars.
That was not the lad I once knew who was killed
In a US air strike.

See, it takes a lifetime to build a future
But only a second to lose it,
Which is why I make the most of every day.
Life is what you make of it
But worth so much more than how so many choose
to live it
And this is where our children are raised.
I'm not even sure if I believe in a god sometimes;
I still pray.

But for me myself,
I refuse to be standing there, arms open,
Should death take a stab at me.
I won't be another number
On the list of kids who faded tragically.

See, I almost died when I was three,
I was one hour from the coffin
When my appendix was removed from me,
So now I can't waste time on death-dicing, acting
stupidly,
For when I see the scar my operation left me with in

scrutiny,
I stand there in my nudity,
Realising how lucky I am to be just breathing.

Between you and me,
Life may be hard but its deeply rooted beauty means
I could never throw it away for something foolishly.
I wish the youth some unity.
God knows we need it when the government
Gives the tower blocks in our council estates
A lick of paint to hide deprivation beneath
aesthetics,
But we're all common as muck so who gives a fuck?
We're born to be arrested or lie on our death beds.

And so many lie on their death beds,
So Rest in Peace:
Jay Kensett, aged sixteen, stabbed to death,
Rest in Peace:
Max Weston, aged sixteen, found critically injured at
the foot of a wall near Ditchling Court,
Rest in Peace:
Deagan Brennan, who hanged himself in his
bathroom at the age of eighteen,
Rest in Peace:
Matt Sadler, aged seventeen, who died when a car
driven by his friend crashed into a garden wall in
Whitehawk estate,
Rest in Peace:
Ollie Golbey, who passed away only days before his
eighteenth birthday in a moped accident,
Rest in Peace:
Connor Saunders, aged nineteen when a single
punch in a fight ended his life,
Rest in Peace:

Lee Rebbeck, aged eighteen, who collapsed outside
a local nightclub and died of cardiac arrest,
Rest in Peace:
Alex Jackson, aged nineteen, who passed away after
a car collision up the road from my house,
And Rest in Peace:
Kyle Burchall, aged seventeen when he took his own
life.

You still talk to us in our dreams, lads.

I write an elegy for the young on the back of the
guns
That we use to prove our adulthood,
I hold an elegy for the young on the back of my
tongue
For every day I will update it.

I pray no more will fill the page,
The future's where our name is.

The future's where our name is.

21ST CENTURY TESTAMENT

When I started turning up to mass
On Christmas Eve only,
When I decided to go carol singing
But for money alone,
When I began praying
For material things and nothing but,
Jesus was disappointed with me.

As the guests at my baptism
Were sinners indeed,
The son of David prayed for me.

But when I replaced Sunday school
With Sunday hangover,
When I stole from my neighbour
And loved my conspirator,
When I took my lady
To a public toilet and loved her prematurely,
The Lamb of God shook his head.

As my boon and indeed my born companions
Were lowly in ambition,
The Second Adam prayed for me.

But when I drank gallons of his blood
At a night club – and mixed it,
When I fed Pride well
And let it mate with Wrath,
When I introduced a Catholic girl to the bedroom
And became, in her eyes, the bastard son of King
Henry,
Jesus was scornful of me.

But I have not forgotten him.
He is invited for a place at the dinner table
When I visit my grandma
And I adore him in a way
That I don't think he understands,
Ah, but I'm too heavy footed
To walk on water,
You are the son of God,
I am the son of a man.

A JOURNEY TO A DESTINATION

The debris by the train tracks is calling to me,
The council flats reach just as high
As the London skyscrapers do
But they slip by just as quick.

It all slips by the window I occupy for the space of
the journey.
I am at peace with the football thugs
Who make their way to the Amex stadium,
Spitting on their hands before shaking.
I know their lives well but I do not alight with them.

I am supportive of the wretched woman
Who reads a book called
How to Get the Little Buggers to Behave.
She is one of those women who tried to be Katharine
Hepburn,
Went wrong and ended up looking more like Pat
Butcher.
I want to let her know she's doing just fine,
But she gets off quickly before I can talk to her.

I feel a warmth towards the crude hen party
With their Doritos tans.
They flail their flabby arms at the ceiling and cackle,
It makes me smile.
One of them leans in to me and says,
'Sorry. They're a bit boisterous.'
I tell her I love boisterous women.
I hope they have a fun night.

I am nostalgic when I see the kids who get on
At St Leonards Warrior Square.
The lads are in tracksuits,
The girls have their hair up in ponytails
And they chew bubble gum loudly.
I was like them once.
They are accompanied by a fat topless bloke with a
pit bull
And a gaunt skinhead.
They're all off to a party in Bexhill.
As they too alight I know I will never see them
again,
They slip away with the lamp posts and vanish into
the night.
It makes me sad in a way
But it was my choice not to go with them.

I come from a culture of terminal jumpers,
I do not get on with ticket inspectors.

I am eager for destination but not impatient,
I know I will get there
No matter which route is taken
Or how many stops are made.

When my hair is grey
And each wrinkle tells a story,
I will remember the faces who alighted years before
And I will love them.

THE NUMBER A

Come, all you cultural pilgrims,
In search of the Number A,
You, who don sweatshop shoes
To attend galas for charities you do not know by
name.

How you have searched for this figure of epiphany,
You, who have scoured the very mountains of Asia
on elephant-back,
Who have scrutinised through binoculars from
theatre boxes
But cannot uncover it in the mass.

You, who worship dead white men
As your school has taught you,
Who wear a toga to the masquerade ball
But find no epic wisdom to your fortune.

You, who sit cross-legged in Bodh Gaya
But reject public transport on the way back,
You, who still do not understand
The lack of grand pianos in council flats.

You, who assume what you search for
Will be written in Latin,
Who are open to enrichment
But selective with compassion.

Oh, how you see yourself reflected in glory
But hang your towel over the mirror wherever you
stay,
How you will hunt, as a short-sighted fool,
That elusive Number A.

FREEZE MEANS RUN

The local prophet taught me that freeze means run,
His eyelids like bindles, well-travelled in England.
He even bought us all fish and chips this once.
He is truly the patron of goodliness.

We caught him in the chippy often,
Debating with himself over a mug of something hot,
Tattooed everywhere but his face, hands and neck,
And that face like potato-rock.

Old artificer of cyclical homes,
He knew us when we arrived after school.
He used to tell us of the joys of having lived in every
city
And the pride in a broken rule.

'Never trust a pig if it's not in a sandwich,
Get to know your rights and keep 'em in your head,
One siren will snitch on you to the other
And everyone wants you dead.

'See a man in the morning before he puts his vest on,
The toast, the orange juice, he is no less human.
Give him a baton, the car and the cuffs,
And tell him that his power is reputed.

'How the flawed change when they think they are
flawless
And the law itself, when you make it lawless.
That's why I tell you freeze means run.
Let it be known from kings to paupers.

'Send them back to their troughs, I say!
Let them squeal with the others!
Cages were not made for men like me,
No, nor you, little brothers.'

And so we went about our days,
All with his motto in mind.
It became the anti-rule rule of the playground
Known in 'It' and in the buff of the blind.

Often we would visit him
In the place chips were prepared
And, as children, three of us could sit where he had
When he came no longer there.

SMALL MAN KINGDOM

My country suffers from small man syndrome.
Goliathan in ego, Napoleonic in height,
He wears clothes twice his size
To try and hide his stature from the other old boys
But they know him too well for this disguise.

My country used to own almost a quarter of the
playground,
And he won't let anyone forget it.
He has left many of his action figures all over it
And now he tries to impress by building his army of
toy soldiers.
He is like a mid-life crisis in a flashy car and with a
small penis.

My country is best mates with a burly lad called
Sam.
He loves him for his muscle; this little brother,
Great, young bulwark, be sensible I beg you,
For so impressionable are these boys at the hands of
each other
That one must keep an eye on the old fire.

THE LAST OF THE MILKMEN

'Is anyone home?' the milkman said
As he rapped upon the door,
Each knuckle grazed and crimson as poppies
From houses tried before.

'Is anyone there?' the man enquired,
Still knocking as he had.
'The milk I left last week is here untouched,
I fear it's gotten bad.'

He lingered for a moment,
But guessing no one home
He set down this week's milk bottle
And turned back to his float.

Not a soul he noticed
But not a care he eyed.
Oh, the blissful virtue
Of his early morning ride.

For as he left by the front garden
He did not catch a glance
Of milk bottles in their abundance
Untouched amongst the plants.

BENIDORM

There's nothing more British than Benidorm.
Upgrade to a luxury suite for a penny more.
Donna is the undisputed karaoke titan,
And Steve has Aphrodite in his bed next door.

Four hundred of those pennies could buy a lager at
the bar
And God knows the fruits of labour come in pint
glasses.
Two thousand of those pennies buy a man
something to smoke,
Elysian fields found in pubs for the masses.

There's nothing more British than Stella Artois.
Bulldogs lick it up from their plastic bowls.
Union Jacks are shaved into the backs of heads
With the patriotism of the old.

There's nothing more British than curry.
Papadums from Luton, traditional Yorkshire mango
chutney,
Murder a cup of tea like George did the dragon
Over a transcendental game of British footy.

There's nothing more British than the Queen,
Nothing more mythological than Germanic ancestry.
The only colours in wardrobes are red, white and
blue,
Clothing British diamonds for the British Diamond
Jubilee.

ROYALS

The construction workers' hats are the crowns of
sacred kings,
Scaffolding – a centurion at the palace gates.
I throw my granddad's overcoat across my sofa
And the New Love Club T-shirt on top of it.

There is a tiger on the streets in my immediate
vision.
I do not think it can see me.
I draw the curtains.
The dumb bells are resting.

The buses crawl on slowly like ships of the Armada,
If I got on one I don't know where it would take me,
But I'd like to one day,
I like adventure.

The bloke cycling past my window rides his bike
with one hand,
He is the refined version of the kids
Who ride their bikes on one wheel
And lean back into the coldness.

They are the children of the florists and chemists
Who drive slowly around Nettleton Road at night.
I have their numbers in my brick T-Mobile.
I haven't called them yet.
They seemed too eager to give me them.

There is a van with the name 'Hoo Hing' sliding
along the concrete.
It will confuse the dole queue Orientalists
Who do not know the difference between China and

Japan.
There are many miscellaneous items in their lofts,
None of it worth much.

She was the queen of tacky junk.
She wore a Burger King crown.
We can't all be part of the royal family.

BOXING GLOVE

I don't know what I write about,
That's for you to tell me.
I don't care how I act at your posh neighbour's
birthday party,
That's for you to do for me.

Secrets are kept to be found out.
There's a lock on my top drawer.
I have left you clues scattered around my flat
As to where the key is.

Search the cabinets.
Is it under the bed?
Or behind the garden gnome?
I do not have a garden.

I operate in nooks and crannies.
Check inside the boxing glove,
Rip it open if you have to,
I am often too temped to use it anyway.

For who am I but the bastard son of subconscious?
I rise with the sun and fall with my enemies,
I wear war paint like the Zulus do.

I am a hardman in front of the lad that wants to do
me in
And keep a key in a hollowed-out hardback book.
I can't remember what it is for.

WESTMINSTER

Do not feed the monkeys
When you come to Westminster, that Gothic zoo.
Instead observe the congregation that stand
By graves dug with abandoned hospital tools.

Ah, Westminster, Westminster!
Troops know not of Ithaca,
Blood in the world's basilicas,
And centuries pass much faster than insolence.

Walking through this city of mammon,
See the rape of foreign soil, the missile penetration,
The wheelchair veterans with tarnished patriotism
And boys that look like machine guns when they
march.

We pay taxes
To fund the wars
That our children die in.

Ah, Westminster, Westminster!
Present to debate your pay but vacant to debate
justice,
Vacant the well-guarded homes of the homeless,
Vacant the poll booth, vacant the rooms when you
appear on television,
Vacant the countenance of the vacant people of the
nation
Who accept vacancy as their sole vocation.

Ah, Westminster, Westminster!
Beyond the pig-head shrines
There be great feasts where elsewhere there be

crumbs.
Imperialist kinsmen
Suck oil from the teat of corruption till numb,
But remember stained lips be eternal.
Walking through Westminster,
See the two wings, only one of which is flapping,
See the ignorant devour from the hands of deceit,
Formal-dress pirates, sword-sharp fearmongering,
Even fish and chip paper will tell you what to
believe
In Westminster!

Aye, but price of the suit does not reflect the brain of
the man –
A lesson to bear in mind in Westminster,
Where miasma-kissed skies, blood orange in shade,
Throw a cover over the innocent.

Some wait by the radio in the kitchen,
Others gather round the television in the shop
window.
Some hear the news carried on bad breath and pale
skin,
Others on flying champagne corks.

I woke to the reloaded five-year reign,
On a dense and maudlin morning.
I lifted my window, I saw the people
And let them hear my calling:

'Ah, once more, Westminster,
A devil can condemn a man to damnation!
How faithful you are, Westminster,
To be home of the country's most notorious
reprobates.

I see you: filthy-fingered miscreants,
Passion-killing philistines,
Bullingdon Club delinquents,
Pride to ash and bastardised,
Ash on every street!

'And you may fill our cradles with it
So we and ash are one at heart,
But, when hated, it is wise to learn
To tell ash and armed man apart.'

BABYLON BIRDS

I

My hell is my haven,
This city of vice is my home.
I occupy the dead space between wake and sleep
In which we pick up our fronts with our shoes.

I occupy space as the birds do,
Beating up against the sky,
Taking the last of the day with them on their wings.
No Babylon can contain the birds.

Every now and then I step out with the sun on my
face
Knowing it is the closest to heaven some of us will
ever get
And how delicate it was before the benefits of love
Touched my life with the sun and put a paradise on
earth.
You can find it if you search,
There is gold in the dirt.

I occupy space known to the return-home workers
And after-school kids who run with mayhem at the
bus stops
And sit at the back seat blaring beats off their bust-
up
Phones, rapping about this and that and 'your
mum's frock'.

And one Year 7 lad, as tall as my elbow,
Takes a seat by his elders in discarded shelltoes,
And a Year 11 lad cocks back his hat,

Looks over the shoulder of this tiny young man
And asks him,
'Excuse me, mate, do you represent the lollipop guild?'
'Fuck off, ya wanker!'

And the sun's still burning for the meantime
As in the fading of summertime
There are still fat blokes walking around topless
Looking like something out of
A 'Builders' Bums of Benidorm' calendar.

As in the fading of the daylight
Young hooligans on mopeds
Are still skidding down the side of Manor Hill,
A grassy bank as steep as the biggest dip in San Francisco is
And I'm at home now.

II

The sunset colour pallet is washing through my bedroom
And the shade is starting to creep in,
The shade is starting to creep in through the sepia
But it doesn't bother me for now.

Ah, because for now I write!
I hold with me one pen and one piece of paper
And all that I am are the words I leave on it
And for many of you that is all you will ever know of me
But need you know anything else?

See, there is a whole world
Just beyond the edge of these rows of houses
And I know because I've heard rumours.
There's an entire world beyond the daylight robbery,
Night-time arrests and headline sodomy
Splashed on front pages like delusions of grandeur.

We have reputations to maintain,
And so we put on a front and act hard,
But this façade is why half of our last star is
darkening.
White lies to save black hearts beget more back
scars,
Taking all or nothing, see the Black Barts bargaining.

Self-annihilation,
Children lacing themselves up with Donkey Dust
and Sniff,
Bhang, Blast, Bath Salts, the thrill of the pill,
The good die young,
The best ain't daft enough to get themselves killed.

And so I write,
Before you wake up I write,
When I'm all on my own I write,
When I'm weak I write,
Lost – I write.
What am I doing in the middle of the night
Whilst the world sleeps tight?
Yes, writing!

I write champagne from silver slippers,
Boxing Day turkey sandwiches.
One day you're king,
The next day you're using sticks to build palaces.

Nothing lasts forever.

Now there are many ways to escape in this world,
Some choose drugs, me – I write,
Some choose drink, me – I write,
So hate me, love me, rate me, begrudge me,
Shoot me on my doorstep,
Just don't dismiss me.
The people that I see every day enrich me
And that is why all the diamonds in the rough
Are sitting atop the ring that I use to marry one city.

And when I write I am no longer here.
If you ever see me writing do not approach me
Because you will soon find out that I am not there,
I am gone, it was never my plan to stay for long,
I write.

And when I write, everything is better,
For just a few minutes absolutely nothing matters,
For just a few minutes I am at peace –
And I know I cannot remain in that place forever
But if I can take just a pinch of it home
It will last me the night.

III

The night,
It's on its way now,
The afternoon is fading now,
The urban foxes will be coming soon.

Some things come all too quickly.
You have told me that patience is a virtue

But for my sins I have little left.

See, sometimes, when the spectrum of daylight is flailing
And falling down on its wavelength, I am stationed
By my window, watching the sun as it chases
The clouds and becomes masqueraded.

And the faces of the people on the streets they are pacing
Are lost like a valuable parcel in mailing,
They're always on the move but they never change places
For as the shops are closing up the mind is raging,
The sunlight still dying out; ah, the last of the milkmen!

Sometimes,
Sometimes I feel.

See, if there's anything I hate more
Than having no time to stop and rest
It's having too much time to stop and rest,
For when I stop and rest
I dance with the burdens I hold on my chest
And I think to myself for our best interest
I wish you'd invest in some actual thought,
Should you frequent my nest and assume I feel blessed
By your presence, I guess we're just guests in our own hearts,
And sometimes I wish we weren't as obsessed,
Sometimes I enjoy when I see you distressed,
See, we refuse to profess what we truly possess,
We repress it instead,

41

And sometimes your happiness I fucking detest!
And sometimes, just sometimes
I really,
Really
Love you.

For among it all,
Among the poor kids who buy bling
Off the rich kids who wear rags for fashion,
Amongst the politicians who think
They're the best thing since the sliced breadline,
Among all of it,
I know I have found something real.

But it is unknown in this land of distortion
So it is feared –
We fear what is real.
I keep myself busy for space leaves time to feel.

IV

So welcome to my city,
When I wander its streets memories come flashing
Like my neighbour in a bath robe,
And keep watch for the kids on London Road;
They leave teeth broken like the Ten
Commandments.

Welcome to my city, mi casa, su casa.
In this hub of cultures
We are surrounded by all sorts like Bertie Bassett
And I love my fellow people
Even if I sometimes hate the place that we inhabit.

And as we reach the end of the day
And come into night
The life doesn't die.

Doner kebabs: the food of the pissed,
Kids having a team piss before they move on from
pre-drinks
To a night that's inconceivable,
An evening full of Candid Camera outtakes,
The result of which – unforeseeable.
'Any excuse to get your kit off, darling, it's more
than agreeable,'
'Is that MDMA or crushed paracetamol?'

While you consider it awhile
Let the night take shape as it billows up against the
clouds
Until it looks like a monster
Breathing out the stars.

The sacred night greets me on a daily basis
But it never tells me its secrets.

While it lurks mysteriously above us,
While it lies luxuriously above us,
The miserable promiscuous and addicted
With dark countenances
Sit on their stoops outside filthy terraced houses,
Everyone watching the ambulance
As it screams away into the city.

For someone's been stabbed,
Someone young, no doubt,
Someone's been stabbed
Again.

And it makes me think.

MEN DON'T CRY

When I was a child I was never fond of dogs.
I've never had a pet in my life, you see.
I'd seen dogs fight in the local park
And I was scared of them, between you and me.

When I was a child, about eight or nine,
My granddad had a dog – an aggressive thing it
was.
We walked it once around a car park by his house
And back across
And it bit me.

Now, my granddad is a hardened bloke
With a working man's pride.
He turned and pretended not to see
As I turned to my mum and cried.

And as he walked his dog
Back through that grey town,
I felt ashamed that I had wept
And let an animal take my crown,
Because men don't cry.

When I was a child, I wore my heart on my sleeve
And faced bullies with cowardice and tears,
But men don't cry, men don't cower
And men may never show fear.

A man is to persevere
Through the jeers and sneers
And other men with spears
Shall never come near a true man.
A man must appear through the war as it clears,

True male, remain unmoved and victorious!

When I was fourteen, I changed – I became a man
And I shunned my tears as weakness,
I made myself a mask
And never showed what was beneath it.

Sometimes, late at night when no one's around
I take it off for a while
And it calms me
But it scares me
So rest assured, when you come home
You will return every time to a stern no-nonsense
countenance
And never something softer.

See, a man's pride is his best and worst quality.
It makes him untouchable,
But not just to pain – to love as well,
For a man can never trust one not to turn into the
other,
And man can never trust trust itself
For if trust betrays him
He may be forced to weep
And men don't cry.

Last month, I went to visit my granddad and as I sat
on the train
I watched young lads getting lairy and testy,
Lads who had probably only just got hair on their
testes,
And I remembered when I was the same.

Last month, I went to visit my granddad,
The dog who had bit me long dead,

And I watched that frail, unhappy old man
And did not look up to him but pitied him instead.

He was a long-time alcoholic
Who had not drunk in years,
Or so I thought, but there I saw,
In his fridge, a beer.

He was not the man he once was.
He was skinnier than before.

His wife had been 'ill' recently,
His insolent, Machiavellian life-sucker of a wife.
She was fine – oh, she was fine – but doted on hand
and foot
By my granddad, as he fetched her lemon drizzle
cake,
Her ugliness only matched by her chain smoking
And constant need to be obeyed.

And my granddad's nervous tic.
I had never noticed that before.

For the minutes my mother and I had alone with
him
He sat there, reminiscing war-time Hunslet
And his own childhood
Before he himself had become a man.

He told my mother and me
That he had not spent enough time with us
And he was too old now to change it
And he wept.

My mother held him; comforted him,
But I, myself, remained seated
And I watched but remained silent.
Nothing but the sight touched my eyes.

What else was I expected to do
When men don't cry?

#POEM

Make sure to always be careful with your words,
Realise that the things you say are heard
And that goes for every tweet and YouTube
comment
Ever made in the whole wide world.

That's your social life; that's where your mates are
at.
Say BRB, return ten hours later,
Well, OMG and KMT,
GCSE English prevailing across the nation.

And I can't promise we'll ever meet again but
I'll monitor how old and fat and ugly you get
Whenever I'm checking my Facebook.
I watch falls from grace like the parents of Amy
Winehouse did,
That's something I can promise.

Be careful not to spend the rest of your life at the
computer.
You'll change.
Your hair will get greasy and you'll start to act ratty,
Hibernate for winter with your pants round your
ankles,
A search history so filthy it would shock Kim and
Aggie,
They'd have to call in the cavalry,
Rubber gloves and everything.

See, video killed radio, DVD killed video,
Netflix killed that, now there's illegal streaming.
Everything becomes as pointless as Yahoo! in the

end.
My PS1 is the only thing I've been keeping,
I'm old-school like that.

So keep cutting and cropping, poking and blocking.
If you have Twitter, consider following your bailiffs.
In this media age it's concerning
Because the writing on the wall round here reads
Brad luvs Chantelle, Gazza woz 'ere
And other such confessions and cultural statements.

Gurns and lemon-suckers,
Wearing flip-flops in snow, hashtag hurry up
summer.

See, the web's been teaching me to swear since
primary school
When I enjoyed saying naughty words like I was
sexting.
It's no use telling children to clean out their mouths
When they don't sell Listerine on Club Penguin.

Club promoters do my head in,
They're cruising for a bruising when they appear on
my inbox
And say, 'Hey, man, cheap entry and hipster bands,
Come down for free shots and them eighties jams.'
Well, fuck you, your launch night and your Essex
tan.

Hashtag swag, hashtag white guys in durags,
Hashtag you're a twat.
Go and Snapchat that.

Hashtag free my mate from prison,
He ain't done shit,
That crack was already sold,
Those necks were already slit.

I live life like a TV blooper,
Inbox full of blackmail, hack your way into
Those government databases and leak what they've
been saying
But only if you can gain asylum in Russia.

Many people would like to tap into my head,
Read my thoughts,
Study my moves
And I'm scared they will.

See, the magic of technology is more than smoke
and mirrors.
It shows the fat girl a pop-up on ways to get thinner
And the chronic wankers methods to make their
dicks bigger,
Techniques that sound like
A Sunday afternoon at Guantanamo Bay.

Which reminds me of the girls on Facebook
Selling themselves for a bill,
Attracting granny bashers, cradle robbers and filth,
A strange lack of ego for an album of selfies
And grimy old bastards unsatisfied by just touch-
screen.

Now I've been getting a lot of emails recently
Telling me I'm the millionth customer,
But I never get my free shit.
I've been thinking a lot about these emails recently

And I'm starting to think they may not be legit.
It does piss me off.

If I could, I would
Delete all the keyboard warriors,
Enter a new space,
Control my escape through word,
Refresh the whole page
And start again.

But God knows we're not there yet.
I'm still careful with my words.

FEMME FATALE

When I come home
My house smells like hard work
And it makes the damp walls unimportant.

I am greeted by a strong woman
Who has been both my mother and my father
And the crumbling bricks are left to erode
Because we are too busy working to leave them
behind.

Never underestimate a woman.
They have untold powers that most men
Are unaware of, but most men
Would malfunction without them.

There is a femme fatale in the film we are watching
To unwind after our day's labours.
I think about the beauty of a femme fatale
(Not in a kinky way but simply appreciative
Of her womanly aura)
And it becomes obvious to me that
I love nothing more than a strong woman.

I think about the olden days,
I mean the really olden days
When women had no rights
But the right to remain subservient
And men were kings clashing
And executing each other
And poisoning each other
And raping each other's women
And I think: damn, those were some strong women!

Then I think about the suffragettes
(The Indian women too –
Sophia Singh is not mentioned enough)
And I think about how they would refuse food in
prison
And how Davison was killed by King George's
horse
And I think: damn, those were some strong women!

My mum used to tell me that bullies are weak
And I think about today as
Women are being blamed for the actions of their
rapists
And little girls see their mothers hit
And even schoolgirls receive sexual harassment
And I know these women but they still smile when I
see them
And that is a power in itself and a strong one at that
And like my mum said, bullies are weak,
So I think: damn, have men ever really been as
strong?

And then I think about the girls I know
With newborn babies
And the fathers aren't around
But the fathers of these girls weren't around either
So they know no different
And it doesn't affect them
And they are passionate mothers and workers
And I think: damn, these are some strong women!

Then I think about my mum
And I look over and my mum has fallen asleep in
her armchair
So I wake her up gently and we go up the dancers

And we say goodnight
And I go into my room
And she goes into hers
And in the morning I wake up early
To make her a cup of tea.

BITTERSWEET EIGHTEEN

Today I turned eighteen
And that means strewn balloons, cake and twelve-
packs of lager
And that means a main course, dessert and a starter.
For breakfast only the full English will do.

And tonight will explode like when propane's lit,
We'll dance the night through on some Soul Train
shit,
Looking dapper, Bobby Dazzler, fresh clothes from
JD and Topman,
My mate's motor is a road rage risk.

We will combine with the hybrid and dance till it's
sunny,
Sweating like bankers in a room full of money.
My mate's on the pull; he's gonna act like a bastard
Because you catch more flies with shit than with
honey.
His fake ID says he's twenty-one.

I, myself, stood there with my passport
And when the bouncer checked it
For the first time in my life I got in
Legally.

I don't know why I was concerned he'd turn me
away.
The bouncer looked at me with a mischievous face.
He looked like Ross Kemp but with an odd hair of
grey.
'Eighteen today… mate.'

'Yes. Eighteen today.'

And then I was struck by exactly what that means,
More than all of those clubs by the beach,
More than being guaranteed service; it means
That my childhood is now over.

No more will I have to loiter at shops
With a nervous excitement on face plastered.
No more will I steal from Sainsbury's self-checkout
And find out if myself or the guard can run fastest.

Today I became responsible.
There are no light punishments now but full
sanctions.
No juvenile, I am accountable for my actions,
No second chances.

And this title of adult is one that will forever stay,
Though I am no wiser than I was yesterday.

Age, yes, you are a delicate flower
In the downpouring rain of time,
And life's short but it's the longest experience you
get
So I'm going to be living mine.

And I am yet to turn twenty but even I have begun
To think that youth is wasted on the young.

We grow up too quick.
Our role models are dealers, thugs and pimps.
We wanna be adults, so by the time we're six
We crave Benson & Hedges with our Panda Pop and
crisps.

But today I turned eighteen,
Today I can drink, today I can smoke,
Today I can gamble, today I can vote,
I am legally a man
But I'm scared like a child.

I'll still do everything I did as a kid, only now I'll do
it legally.
On that day that I turned eighteen
I became what the children dream to be,
The only dream that's ever really certain to come
true.

On that night, we shared the same drinks and dance
floor
But we lived in different worlds,
For I groom and maintain the run of my time
While my friends ride it in prison cells.

See, age is both the biggest buzzkill
And the biggest excuse for fun,
Because when we're young
We can use the excuse we don't know better
To get away with whatever we want.

And when we're getting on we'll blast modern
songs
That we secretly don't like
And drive around all night having a mid-life crisis
Trying to be twenty-five.

One day we will be too old
To only be young once.

Yesterday I was a rebel without a cause,
Tomorrow I'll be round the bend,
Today I turned eighteen,
Today and never again.

A NOTE FOR DAHLIA

He plucked that flower
When it had not fully grown.
Many years of sunlight left she had,
Deep rooted in the soil of home.

But he plucked that flower for she was pretty,
Undressed the petals with nimble fingers
And stole her back to his part of the city,
Then, when she wilted, left her alone.

He had a book of pressed flowers –
Amongst the buttercups and hydrangeas
There lay Lilies, Roses, Daisies, Veronicas
And many more crushed with names unknown.

Have you ever seen a flower that stood up in court
Amongst the deafening mallet and muttering teams?
Such place as this unfit for one so young,
A strong flower she was, indeed.

'There is no evidence this flower's been plucked.'
Leave the witness box in tears; return to the mud of
home.
Many more blossoms are in danger as of tonight
But now she has a flower of her own,
A beautiful baby girl.

Dahlia was her child's name; watered daily with
love
And raised by her flower-mother alone,
Her first taste of sunshine equally sweet
To those with two to help them grow.
And at primary school

Dahlia's grades are predicted
Before she touches the playground earth,
All based off her parents: 'are they single or double?'
But who's to say any child is better
Than her?

And at secondary school,
On the night of the prom,
She sees groups of flowers in dresses of material
worth,
But, Dahlia, yours is richest simply for being on you.
Who's to find a cotton finer
Than hers?

Dahlia, you will grow as nature intends,
Though you have had to be an adult from birth,
And though once wilted, your mother is the
strongest of flora.
I thank God that she has found, by you, mirth.

And this is just a note I am leaving you, Dahlia,
Though support has never been something your
mum or you need.
How you have blossomed! You are a woman,
Dahlia!
(And what woman better than she?)

POETS ARE ENDANGERED

'Poets are endangered,' he tells me.
'Take away their celery sticks
And hummus and butterfly nets,
Stitch blood stains into
Their clogs and tweed jackets,
The children don't want you anymore.

'They no longer want to learn about you.
Poets are not suited for modernity.
Wordsworth does not have his own Vevo page.
I have never seen Milton on MTV Cribs.

'Poets are endangered,' he says.
'Crash their tour coach into the Sussex Downs.
If a poet dies but no one's there to see it
Did they ever really exist?
The brave new world is not fit for such people,
Another poet gone with each tree that hits ground.'

'Well, well, well,' I reply,
'What lyrical language for someone that hates
poetry.
There are some flaws in your words.
Do not yet put the nail in the coffin,
Do not yet bring round the hearse.

'You will not catch me making a daisy chain,
Nature is not what I follow,
These archaic archetypes are far from current
But you have overlooked the poets of tomorrow.

'See, we are the poets of the city,
We know what the bottom of the butter tub looks

like,
Flowers do not grow well where we come from.
You cannot measure modern heroes by heroic
couplets
As you cannot judge a sordid romance at the club
By a panegyric love song.

'In this new world of delusional grandeur
The youth need something real
And whilst they may not pick it up in school-time
textbooks
It is them to whom the new poets appeal.

'We are the ones who raise your children
When they are sick of trivial media.
We are the ones that nurture their voice.
To no form are we obedient.

'Drop the pansy politics.
I have written poetry with ex-cons,
I have made drug dealers cry,
I have seen poetry in lyrics
Exchanged in rap battles at lunchtime.

'Drop the softie stories.
Our slang is our weaponry.
I could write a lampoon just for you
And it could last for centuries.

'I have seen poetry sprayed in paint on walls,
I have taught poetry to those who used to tease me
for it.
Thank you, new world, for making classic books so
cheap.
Every day we are bettering and maturing.

'We have sharpened our minds as we have our
pencils,
Uncensored and not giving a fuck.
The poets are far from endangered.
If anything, the poets are waking back up.'

SEASIDE POSTCARD

Take me to the shore,
Take me to the middle ground between civilisation
and unexplored depth,
Where the children will learn to love the bruises on
their feet
And disregard anything but pebbles on a beach.

Take me there most any time,
I want to wade in the water during a thunderstorm
And there's always a bloke with his top off in the
dead of night
But most will come out when the sun is warm.

There you will see the tracksuit lads on their
mopeds
Pacing the same roads that leather jackets and suits
Had clashed on fifty years earlier.

Here in our 'utopian-in-its-own-way' Atlantis,
Beers bellies are romance
And they are exhibited with British pride and
prowess.
Greasy foreheads, sweat and spit are championed
In this Shakespearian Benidorm.

Everyone's trying to get on someone,
Here in paradise anything goes,
Half of us are either pale or sunburnt,
They say the saltwater tastes best in the undertow.

This season belongs to Slush Puppies and
doughnuts,

The girls in string vests with skin-tight cornrows,
And an attempt to take your portable speakers out
On a knackered blow-up rubber boat.

'Sun's out, guns out,' the gym men say,
Flex your biceps if they're big enough to feel.
This doesn't apply to the man who thinks he looks
like Arnold Schwarzenegger,
But looks a tad bit more like Ian Beale.
He hasn't been eating his Brussels sprouts and
Shredded Wheat.

This day belongs to the bleach blondes with brown
wrinkled skin
And the Dick Turpin seagulls who nick your chips,
It belongs to the morning-after-Gay-Pride hangover
warriors
And the hen party in the same clothes they wore for
last night's stint.

They all go to bars and drink Sex on the Beach,
Then daydream about having sex on the beach.

Burnt skin chocolate on tanned skin strawberry on
pale skin vanilla,
Our tan lines make us look like Neapolitan ice
cream.
Salty candyfloss, doughnut vinegar,
A luxurious fish-and-chip hedonism exclusive to
Blighty.

One Cornetto
And a dash of Amaretto.
My mate thinks the drinks are cheapest at Asda
But we always end up going to Tesco.

A sightseeing bus full of miserable pensioners,
All of them squinting in the sun,
Moves among the bumper-to-bumper cars
With boots full up of water guns.

A tattooed leg sticking up in the distance.
Who really pays for deck chairs?

A skinny kid is surveying the whole beach cynically,
Blue and green ice cream running down ginger
freckled arms.
A girl tells a lad she's sweeter than candyfloss,
He tells her he's harder than rock
And makes the most of his natural charm.

Now, you can never be certain of British weather,
So whenever it's hot we forget where our clothes
are.
We walk to the shore with our bodies hanging out,
Basking in the highs without a care what the lows
are.

This is how summertime has always been
And there's nothing more stunning to have at your
home's heart.
If I can't be there with you one year
You'd better make sure you send me a postcard.

FRED

The youth were born for the future.
They were not born to follow the scars of their
fathers,
Imitate the tears of their mothers,
They were just raised by them.

One finger on the point of identity,
Traced from a birth certificate
Through mud on its journey.

My lad, my lad,
My great-granddad Fred bought
Apples and pears from the market,
Then sold them off again for a profit
And ended up owning a fruit shop regardless
Of his class and youth.

Why sell drugs, my lad?
My lad, do not let Monopoly money seduce ya.
If life gives you lemons, sell the bloomin' things.
The youth were born for the future.

I'd like to see the Prime Minister in a soldier's hat.
We will not turn to stone pawns when you stare at
us.
Your name is not David Medusa.
The youth were not made for war, you prat,
The youth were born for the future.

My lad, my lad,
My great-granddad's friend got in debt to Yorkshire
gangsters.
My great-granddad went out to his house

And they stood at the top of his landing.
He told his friend, 'Boil water in pans.'
When the mobsters broke in they stood waiting.
'Whoever comes first gets this scorching liquid on
his head.
Who's it gonna be? We'll be patient.'

Now, my great-granddad detested crime
But those gangsters thought he was ruthless.
You don't have to be a crook to be a badman.
My lad, the youth were born for the future.

One thing about my great-granddad Fred is he
never left the country,
But he read all the encyclopaedias,
So he could tell you about geography.
He left school at the age of twelve,
But he could teach you about geometry,
Philosophy and trigonometry.

Because the youth were born for the future
And although young men are laid to earth each year
(A British hospital two-hundredth to be faithfully
trivial),
You hear the voice of reason if you don't turn deaf
ears.

And I may never have met my great-granddad
But he is not my male role model in vain,
For my mother named me
Thomas Frederick Sissons;
I carry this man in my name.

Now, one thing more
(And I bet you this):

If my great-granddad was still here now,
He'd tell me, 'Well, do whatever suits yer,
But I don't see why you focus on me;
I'm the past.
The youth were born for the future!'

THE OLD FORT

Unknown secrets are here,
Untouched realms of peace and harmony are here.
They whisper in the breeze, much like the distant
hollering of the children
Who tread the beach rocks without the fear of their
feet being cut;
It is all carried in the wind.

Here in this old fort,
Where battles were waged long before our existence,
Nobility and pride went hand in hand for England.
Among these ruins, where all is left lingering in the
dusk,
Men who feared not to shed blood
Watched the sea at the very brink of their homeland
And fell in its defence.

They are the forefathers of the boys
Who fear not to shed blood for different reasons,
Pride and integrity all the same
But they fall at the hands of those who live on the
same street.

Beyond the legend of these untouched ruins,
Those who have never seen them
Perish for their phones and their trainers:
Objects upheld with as much pride as countries
And dead men who fell for this all silent.

To forget such places,
Such untouched reminders,
Is to forget much more than history.

Across the harbour waters,
Fluttering in the very same breeze
That whispers in the Old Fort,
A flag old and decrepit.

There are secrets here,
Untouched realms of peace and harmony are here.
They whisper in the breeze much like the distant
hollering of the children
Who tread the beach rocks without the fear of their
feet being cut;
It is all carried in the wind.

GANGSTERS

Mummy, when I grow up I want to be a gangster,
I want to pop bottles in the club and leave with
twenty girls.
I was taught how to fight by Ryu and Blanka.
I was force-fed MTV Cribs.

Mummy, I wear my ASBOs like badges of honour
But I need to up my game to get the new Lexus.
It's all well and good robbing kiddies in the street,
But I have dreams of being in the Ten Most Wanted,
The Ten Most Respected.

'What sort of dreams are these?' you ask me.
These are the dreams of my generation, Mum.
They come in two forms: cash and reputation.
Working in the supermarket won't get me either
one.

'What's given you dreams such as these?' you ask
me.
Well, they show us happiness via the mansions on
the TV screen,
But when we reach for this joy and our hand strikes
the glass
It reminds us that these are carrot-on-string dreams
And are as distant as they could ever be,
But now we want them even more.

See, they feed us and starve us at the same time.
Those who teach us regard us as born to do crime,
So why should I let them down? They're right,
right?
Even police have harnessed a taste for violence,

They have printed it on the eyelids
Of Mark Duggan and Ian Tomlinson.
Did you expect me to turn out any differently?
I was raised around young gods clashing Trident.
It's either me or them, Mum,
So don't ask me what I have in my pocket.

See, the government want to crack down on crime,
But meanwhile they are gangsters themselves.
Our estates lie adjacent to the silver-spoon
penthouses.
We turn green when we see them, green as a note,
And they use us as if we were money ourselves.

So we become the dummies of record labels
Or back-breaking work
And do whatever they tell us we should,
Whether that be explicitly in the form of a contract
Or implicitly projected in materialist songs
To every young man in a hood.

Mummy, when I grow up I wanna be a gangster.
I wanna whine with a girl who lives round the way,
Take a photo and send it to her man's best friend.
I want to hear my boys scream out, 'Free me, free
me,'
If I have to ride a bird in the pen.

Mum, there's something romantic about the name
Kray,
And Escobar and Capone.
Mum, you've always told me I should have male
heroes
And I ain't had no dad to look up to at home.

Mum, I was made for this.
I remember storing sweets up behind my teeth
For practice – I've always known what I've wanted
to be.
I want to hear my boys scream, 'Free me, free me,
free me,'
Mummy, free me,
Free me,
Free.

LIONS FROM ANTS

I hold protest in one clenched fist.
Should I pump it I would be raising the very power
Which can overthrow palace walls, usurp dictators
And make lions out of ants.

I have heard war cries,
I have known them to be nailed to the doors of
churches,
I have known them to banish monarchs to foreign
lands
And I have observed them in their thousands.

I have observed tens of hundreds of thousands
Roaring in communities which belong to them in
morals but not in laws,
The country which hosts their beating heart but
rejects their voice
And hears screams in return.

Let your children listen to them,
Pick out their words if you can.
It may be difficult for they are deep within
The uproar of chants which are sewn together in
uncoordinated unison.

Sewn as tightly as the finest garments or rugs
Which remain on the floors or in the wardrobes
Of the Olympians' homes.

Read them as you would the finest literature.
They have become known to you in history books
As wondrous fancies,
Mythological figures unfed on the dusty bookshelf.

The mothers and fathers of the unfulfilled or
unappreciated,
Thousands of years and still they live,
After our deaths still they will strive
And be born again at the dawn of each new bill, ban
or law,
Each crying in their mother's arms with differing
appetites.

They are lions in a flimsy cage,
Bulls in an everlasting sea of red.
Do you hear them?

HYMNS OF RAGNARÖK

Ah, Mr Down-and-Out, sing a hymn for me,
Retire into the flames the weary urchins
Who are not pretty enough
To be seen on television screens.

Mr Down-and-Out, you knew the end was always
dawning,
You begged us for a penny but the smallest we had
was 10p,
Another cycle of the sun spent empty,
With expensive possessions we can never take with
us
Crammed into lofts, bedrooms and garages.

Captives die for the pirate flags that imprison them,
Stockholm Syndrome populations,
The borders of our nations engulf in flame,
They were made of matchsticks all along.

And they never saw the end until it struck them in
the face
Like their mothers with a wet flannel on a church
Sunday morning,
Mr Vicar-man, can't you say a prayer for me?
Hope usurps certainty.

On the Judgement Day, parliaments have emptied,
Those glued to their sofas are ripped from them
And thrust for the first time out into nature
In its cataclysmic glory.
A catalyst of seven billion,
Grains of sand have bought about the apocalypse
And not even favourite celebrities

Will survive Ragnarök.

Ah, Mr Down-and-Out, sing a hymn for me,
The prophecy was written on your face all along.
How blind can visionaries be?
Forgive us, disregarded messiah.

REPRESENT

Where do you represent?
In which part of your city do you fly your flag?

When we were lads we represented where we came
from
With graffiti sprawled on the walls of our
neighbours' houses.
Faces of Ozymandias,
Look upon our kingdom.
It stretches from that chip shop, round by the pub
And back up to the dilapidated terraced houses,
Where abandoned street sofas are our thrones.
See our mighty empire and be fearful.

My older friends, local brethren of childhood,
Represented our area in a car outside the cemetery,
In the bareness of winter, wearing the same old
tracksuits
And waiting hours for a customer.

The neighbour boy, he represented our area
By taking an air rifle into our school
And shooting it off in the face of a thirteen-year-old
kid.
Neighbour boy, what have you done
For where you come from by this?

Neighbour boy,
To promote where we're from by destroying our kin
Is how we represent
What we fear is not worth representing.

Neighbour boy,
It has been years and I've grown to a man.
All my childish behaviour is spent.
I no longer care about where you proclaim,
I now care about what you represent.

And don't tell me
It's the sportswear brands that enslave you,
Don't tell me it's the new phone, the new game,
It's old news, I told you, my friend,
There is more to life than this
But there is someone out there
Who sees us as one big mound of dirt
And he doesn't want us to realise it.

So tell me now, will you really represent
Or will you carry on killing our children
Until none of them are left?

If you pick the latter,
Then you may stand there,
Amidst our once-inhabited houses,
Arms spread, and cry out,
'Look upon my kingdom!'
It now stretches through empty streets
And the gutters are littered with
Past relics of bygone times
When there was still hope for us,
A football as punctured as the heads of your foes
And now no one remembers these roads,
'See my mighty empire and be fearful!'

Neighbour boy,
Where have you gone?

Neighbour boy,
When I go from city to city
Spreading my words:
That is how I represent!
When I tell the council who I am
And what I stand for:
That is how I represent!
When I go to underprivileged schools
(The same schools we went to)
And teach the kids of the next generation:
That is how I represent!
And what's more,
I will not die for the place I was born;
I want to make the place I was born worth living for.
That is how I represent!

And when I go back home
To the place I come from,
The people who never left it recognise me
Though my face no longer blends with the tarmac
And I will sit and have drinks as I used to
With the people I will always love,
Who still occupy the houses to the chip shop and
back.
And I will tell them:

'This is where we were raised
But this is not for what we were meant.
We are not just what we are born as,
We are how we reinvent.

'But I will always cherish the place
Where I realised this at length,
For this is not just where I come from,
This is what I represent.'

YES, GROWTH, BUT STILL
(The Yeses and Buts of Maturity)

I'm older than I was a minute ago
And in that time I've matured.
I keep bank statements in my shoebox now,
I've cleared out the toy guns of before.

Some may say I've been reborn,
But I haven't really; I've just matured.
My eyes haven't changed,
My personality not too much either.

I still count dust bunnies,
Just beneath a different sofa.
I still wish I could pay for things with Monopoly
money,
But now it's rent and not a brick Motorola.

I still like to hear about the dripping bread days
In Yorkshire on my mother's side
And I still enjoy a pie and Bovril,
Because it keeps me warm inside.

I still get fast food when I've been drinking
But now I know how to control myself when I'm
drunk.
I still think school never taught me much
But now I regret the days that I bunked.

I'm older than I was a minute ago,
In that time I've matured,
And though years are but seconds on the face of the
earth
Find eternal the burning core.

LATIN

I use Google Translate to learn Latin.
Discere Latinam utor Google Translate.

EXHIBITIONISM

If I keep your photo face down on my bedside table
But do not remove it,
Is it art?
If I start to wear thick-rimmed glasses
When my eyesight is not failing me
In order to stay loyal to utmost irony,
Is it art?
If I start every piece with the sentence:
Your whole life has led up to you reading this poem,
It is true, but is it art?
If I sketch my name into your car
With my house keys
Or draw a smiley face on the Mona Lisa
And call it iconoclasm
But avoid explaining why
Or write gullible on your forehead with a permanent
marker,
Don't be angry,
Is it art?

Statues of refugees in ivory or blackwood
Or in boats as underwater sculptures –
A metaphor to be observed by the most cultured
fish,
Photos of those you could be feeding,
Women with shaved heads,
Art?

If I hibernate inside into my middle ages
And watch my hairline fade in the mirror
And keep a gun in my drawer
And if the neighbour kids are scared of me
And if no one comes to visit me

Am I art?

There is a frequently misconstrued difference
Between art and artful.

To subvert the bastion of the social elite
Like what the chavs did to Burberry,
I call that an art.
At the same time
The celebration of marginality
Is an art.
The craft of cutting hair,
Unblocking a sink, fixing a boiler,
Sweeping a street is an art.

I would love, if I could,
To immortalise these artists
In Greek marble or alabaster.
I would sell them to museums
And share the money amongst the models
And all the Hellenistic torsos
And the stately figures in bronze
And Venetian red
Would wonder what's going on.
But then everyone would think it was cool.

A MAN WHO'S COME TO TOWN

There is a man who's come to town.
He has the ability to seduce both your daughter and
your son.
He brings with him a storm cloud of infatuation
And rests one foot on the head of love.

There is a man who's come to town.
People dare dream to lay him out on their bed.
He brings with him deceit amongst crooks
And assassination amongst royalty.
He walks through the most deprived areas
But leaves when all are dead.

There is a man who's come to town.
He will make your son sell drugs for him.
Your daughter stands on the corner for him.
He brings with him everything we think we need
And everything we think is worth dying for
And all statuses to fall to his whim.

There is a man who's come to town.
He will lead you to think he makes men out of
animals
But then shortly after he makes animals out of men.
He brings with him what we think is power,
But count this man;
He may be worth less than you expect.

ALGEBRA

We both know trouble like the backs of our red
hands,
We etch it into tables with flick knives or scissors
That we should have been using
To cut out geometrical shapes.

I am one who learns more at the gates,
Where pupils circle on bikes with drawstring JD
bags
That would be confiscated if the teachers knew
What was inside them.

Incomprehensible comprehensives.
We do not wear uniforms how they were tailored to
be donned,
Ties low at our chests, blazers inside out
Like the way the Fresh Prince taught.

I grew up with a school of thought,
Not an academy of education.

Yet again Sir is eyeing up his occupation,
Quick to lose his patience, he waits for a kid to test
him
(White-knuckled) and then punches him in the
corridor
Like it will teach him algebra.
Meanwhile we live through rhythm and music,
Gaining identities through basketball court rap
battles,
Football feuds, quick fists,
Tobacco begging and soggy prison rollies.

The girls achieve it much quicker via the use of
chicken fillets,
Everyone hates Jamie Oliver for wanting to make us
thinner
And daydreams are broken by Chinese burns
And heads down toilets.

The lads who carry shanks:
We went to school with them.
Make sure you stay cool with them
And when the bus driver goes to break up a fight
And they steal his money,
Avert your eyes.

We went to GCSE exams with notes on our hands
And we still don't know our times tables,
But don't fret; there are books in the local library.
I, for one, will be teaching myself,
For I did learn to read at least.

I grew up in a school of thought,
And whilst it had not the material goods to be
elitism,
It had not the weakness to be defeatism.
It was a solidarity we all felt
And I pray it will make us better adults
In the long run.

For when I teach poetry at failing academies,
These pupils, with their ties low at their chests
And their blazers inside out,
Are all asking questions
And raising their hands
With no middle fingers or nothing.

I WANNA WRITE POEMS
(A Homage to Steve Colman)

I wanna write poems
But not just any poems,
Poems that you don't just hear but feel,
Poems that outlive their writers in sacred texts
For the undying messages they conceal.

Poems that your grandchild's grandchild will study.

Poems of a scorching summer metropolis,
Memories of childhood, after-school SNES,
Innocent schemes to get rich through a car-washing
business
That gained 20p per head.

Football hooligan thug poems,
Coffee bar beatnik love poems,
Down-and-out soup and crust poems,
Old wives' tale bed bug poems,
I wanna write more poems.

I wanna learn sign language
So I can write the deaf poems
And, for the blind, converted-to-Braille-text poems.
In my next poem, I wanna show those
With the weight of the world on their shoulders
A get-it-all-off-your chest poem.

A tell your mother, your sister and your missus
poem,
A rhythmic poem, not a sit there, be preached at and
listen poem,
A get-with-it poem,

So sugary sweet, your tooth needs a filling poem.

That's a swinging poem,
A hazy afternoon chilling poem,
Slang-filled lyric poems,
A wheeler and dealer on the straight and narrow,
'This year I'm gonna make an honest killing' poem.

I wanna write the poem of the next revolution,
Boxing glove poems that deliver blows
And knock the wind out of stomachs – like Eliot
Ness,
Poems that make you feel untouchable
As if you were wearing twenty layers of vests.

Poems of the voice of the modern Renaissance.

I wrote this poem on the back of my hand,
I wanna write poems on the body of a beautiful
woman,
I want this poem to go further than human voice,
I want this poem to be carried out in the wind
currents.

A love-each-and-every language poem,
Never a guerrilla-militia propaganda poem.
They say the pen's mightier than the sword
So if they come for me
All I need is a biro and a poem.

I wanna write superhuman poems
With unlimited powers
And my aching hand knows I've just finished a
poem,
But it will only fill my craving for limited hours.

Your mates will never guess
Who's just written
A poem
Again.

GOD WAS A POET

Worship me not,
I am no different from you.

I too am the child who lost his sandcastle
When the tide came in,
I too lie for a while staring at the ceiling
Every morning when a new day begins.

Fear me not,
I am no bigger than you,
Just older –
Older and weaker.
I made each patch of grass equally sacred
And not the slight bit greener.

Do you remember nature?
You haven't seen it for a while now
And you have been warring for my name,
But you slay your father's children,
And litter my garden with their graves.
Was no one there to tell you 'thou shalt not kill'?

Ah, but I suppose I gave you free will,
I created the earth in which you may ebb and sigh,
Fall and weep,
Laugh and rise as you please.
I had only prayed you would live and grow
Like the flora does.

I gave you my trust
But surely it is my fault you have abused it,
For I have been careless in my creation
And storms and fire

Have replaced homes with rubble and pyres.
I made my sandcastle in too much haste,
I thought myself wiser than was true
And that is why I say I am no higher than you.

I am not shocked you denounce my existence.
From out my flaws the flaws of Man have been
driven.
Perhaps it is best you denounce my existence,
Worship me not, worship what I have given.

Do you remember nature?

ARMY ANTS

Such grounded men watched from an aerial view.
As the bird glares down at people,
The people gather on bridges and look over at the
railway workers
In bright-coloured uniform like insects on an eternal
stretch.

Yes, they are at work again.
They start before you leave your bed in the morning
And finish long after you lay your hat up at night,
Great, sweaty army ants of labouring Infrastructure.

They are in the sewers shovelling your waste,
They are in the docks loading your goods
And in the streets collecting your bins.
Their clothes may be mauled by oil and grime
But their blue collars are kept cleanly on display
With trophy-hall pride.

They have set up a club,
Solidarity for army ants.
They have elected leaders from around the country.
'Stop these crushing conditions.
We are not paid per drop of sweat but per bucketful
of it.
Coinage trickles down the pyramid
But is never what it was at the top
By the time it reaches the bottom,
But ignorant are those who sit at the peak,
For think what happens to the whole of that
pyramid
When the ants walk away from holding it up
underneath.'

Recognise the mandibles.
Understand the glory of the funiculus,
Worthy femurs and well-seeing compound eyes.
Do not underestimate the tarsal claw.

Ants to some they may be,
But their shadows behind them
Are cast as great as those
Who are made statues of.

TRAP-HOUSE HONEYMOON

'My lady,' said the crack-addled hero to his girl,
'Let us go on a trap-house honeymoon.
We have no bags to pack,
All is sold but the clothes on our back
And these are threadbare at best,
So let us go on a trap-house holiday.

'The people may clock us from a distance
In our four-foot stagger-waltz around the trap-
house,
Me singing the ballad of the baritone addict
Clutching you to my heart
So you can hear how you too speed it up.

'Imagine you spinning on your heels
In all the elegance you can muster.
People may point,
They may call you that mephedrone ballerina
And the pigeons may shit on us.

'Groups of girls may giggle at us as they flock by
And mothers may grip their children's hands
And the old men may avoid our gaze
And lower the brims of their hats
As they continue up the street

'But we will come together there,
Me with this ratty old moustache,
Grease-clumped hair and weasel face,
You with your golden teeth,
Crop top miniskirt combination,
Muddy knees (I'll wash them later)
And voice like the scratch of a vinyl

(My favourite part of the listening)
And we shall sing our wedding song
Before we go in.

'When we reach the door
I shall pick you up
If my weak arms will allow me
And we shall kiss.

'Then by the light of the cracked glass
And the exchange of needles,
We shall be man and wife
And none the more sovereign.

'They may say what they want
And act as they do
But, my lady, we are in a better position.
We have everything to gain
And nothing to lose.

'My lady, if you will have me,
I'll be happier than all else in that room.
We have nothing to pack and no home to leave,
Our love by a silver spoon.'

TO WEAR A SUIT

I have read somewhere that the reason
Trains have such ugly patterns on their seats
Is to hide the fact that they're all filthy.
I sit on months, even years of grime
On the way home from monotony.

When I first got my hands on those second-hand
millionaire's shoes
I thought I was proper fancy,
But I can't show them off anymore by crossing my
legs
Because they're scuffed (plus, I'd look unmanly).

Besides, I am a labourer.
I carry crates of champagne so maybe one day I can
drink from them.
When they take the wine from my tray, have a sip
and put it back
I think they must not know what I can bring to
them.

But oh, they will see me soon,
For I have a second-hand suit
And my granddad's NABC tie too.
I still have scuff marks on my shoes
But I can fit into my smart trousers
Now that I've lost some weight.

When I wear my suit,
Some may confuse me for those I carry trays for,
But if they do, I make sure I speak to those people,
I make sure they hear my voice,
For I will not let them mistake me.

TAYO'S STARS

I

Stars can be dangerous things
If you cross them a certain way.

Since the days of divorce and birthday cake,
Tayo had always had a glint in his eyes.
It was the first thing people would notice about him,
The impish grin of a naïve child.

His mother used to show him the African stars
Before they came to this kingdom of Albion.

They rest up there in the constellations
Held by the hand of God in a glove,
On thrones of the globe, white-hot to touch,
Looking down on the poorest like a dominant love.

Tayo had always longed to grasp those stars,
He prayed to play amongst them for he knew not
how.
He got impatient waiting for the Lord to reply
And so he resolved to turn instead to the local cash
cow.

Because the schools couldn't teach,
Religion couldn't preach,
Minimum wage was not raised,
So the people couldn't eat.

And Tayo could spend years
Searching for a chance to stack shelves
Or Tayo could make a grand in a week

On his own street.

No one had ever taught him
How to climb to the stars,
So Tayo resolved to bring the world down around
him,
Until they fell with it and into his palms.

Drugs is the word; he saw it as a business
In an all-black suit with bags of white and green.
He could buy his mum a necklace and repay her
debts,
He was more than he could hope for; he was
nouveau-riche.

Ah, the stars were smiling on him then,
But it wasn't long till his mother found the bags in
his shoebox.
She disowned him, turned him out and lowered her
head.
What could she do when Tayo was too far gone?
She must focus on the future of her younger children
instead.

So from hostel to hostel, Tayo would drift
And when he tasted his failure, he learnt how to
spit.
He began to lose clients cutting salt into bags.
Desperation wore his face in cash-losing fit.
He found himself owing money to gangs of
treacherous hands
So he abused his own products to calm himself
And when he did he was happy, so he never looked
back.
After two months, his mate took him in,

He handed Tayo shelter for as much time as needed to be spent,
Food, drink and somewhere to rest his head.

Ah, that once-open, dream-filled head.
Under a night sky where those stars grew red,
Tayo lay awake turning, rotting and burning
Until the whole house slept
And then he stole everything.

The hand that feeds bitten and gnawed off at the wrist,
Once-open palms became disfigured fists
But Tayo saw only pound signs before him
When in a craze he robbed all the things
That his sleeping friend would have been willing to give
And ran.

But the thing about Tayo's mate was this –
He could never allow himself to be taken for a prick,
So when he woke up to his ghost of a home
He knew that a throat was going to be slit.
He called up the men to whom Tayo owed money
And told them to bring their stones and their sticks.
'We've given him time, now we'll give him the bricks,
His bones will be broken; his dome will be split.'

So they followed Tayo from city to city,
Two trains and a bus and each boy equipped,
Five with blades tucked under their sleeves
And one with a black star nine by his hip.

And I heard of how they did ride by his lips,

How they'd taken that glint from the young boy's
eyes
And not forgetting that impish smile
From his lips.

That night the stars were further away
Than they had ever been.

II

It was no more than two weeks later,
When the sky was asleep in the wake of the storm
And my midnight walk took me through the train
station.
Leisurely I trod its deserted platforms.

It was a no man's land
Enclosed in barbed wire shrubbery.
No water under the bridge here,
Just tracks.

That day had seen a downpour unmatched by the
Amazon,
And the world was still strewn with the tears of the
sky,
As if a massacre in heaven had burdened the earth,
Lifeless and rain-beaten as the figure
That now emerged and approached from the dirt.

Dishevelled as a waif, ragged as an urchin,
Unkempt hair where strict cornrows had roamed,
The tip of a knife that glistened

Similar to the spark that had ignited the eyes of
Tayo's.

It was him.

He demanded my money,
But I found myself aware
Of the fact that I wasn't scared.

For I remembered the time when we used to break
bread
When we thought we ran the city
Because we overran the city –
The journey we had shared as men,
So it did not matter that he didn't recognise me:
One of his oldest and dearest of friends.

So I emptied my wallet
And he snatched my money like I held the stars
themselves
And before he left, he gave me that impish grin,
The grin I had not seen for so many years.
Even now I still treasure it.

He was sweet sixteen and I saw that night
That he had allowed himself to take his own life.
He was too far gone to be saved.
The Tayo I'd known had been dead for so long a
time.

Consider the sky.
We must be careful when approaching that illusive
land
For in grasping at stars we may burn our hands
But we'll still find a way; it may take time

But we must not be impatient with the road we have
planned.

Tayo had tried from so young an age,
From days of divorce and birthday cake,
But on that night, in the war-torn blackness
I noticed something had left in his wake.

I did not say a word,
I acknowledged it only with eyes,
Then I turned back and headed home
Under a starless sky.

NECESSITIES

When I am old
(And God willing I live to be so),
I should very much like to be
More young at heart.

Would I stay in the city?
Yes, I think so,
But, at weekends, visit
Countrysides and parks.

I should like to have a wife
I have known since a youth
Who still loves me when I have
More wrinkles than sense.

We shall go on vacations
To Butlin's in summer
And keep for the homeless
Each spare pence.

And she shall look as beautiful
In her wedding dress
As she ever did.
If I was rich
(And I could either take it or leave it),
I would still cherish the times
I had nothing.

I would read to my grandchildren
All that I've written
And, whether they like it or not,
They will love it.
For when my children, Teddy and Dolly,

Have heard all my stories on many a day,
I shall require the ears of Bertie, Elsie and Sonny
To listen afresh to what I have to say.

To love and write and read good books
Is all I find I need in the end,
And should you knock on my door
Years from now when I'm old
You'll find me loving, writing, reading again.

GOODNIGHT SON

The day has been long,
The night will only be longer
But I am here with you,
My son.

In this night, you may find things changing,
Colder indeed and we may see our breath in our
own house
But remember, I am here for you,
My baby.

Our bed will always be warm.
Aye, we may have to kick our legs around to heat it
up
But we are blessed, you and I,
And basics are enough.

Goodnight, buggerlugs,
Dream of sweet peace till the morning.
In this night you may see the boys you once knew
Who have risen, conquered and fallen.

But be not scared,
For they are mere shadow puppets on the ceiling,
And you will not find them unless you call them
out.
It is you that keeps their hearts beating.

So dash the riches,
Dash the finery and dash what the pompous believe,
Indulgence and luxury
But two thinly veiling sheets.

And should you find yourself
An adult in comfort with your needs,
Be glad, but let it be known of all
That died on childhood streets.

Goodnight, babsyhead,
Let's lay the story book down
And I shall hold you tight till you sleep
Despite who laughs or frowns.

In this night, just remember the beauty of the world.
It is not there when you search for it but you will
find it instead
In the least likely of places
And directly ahead.

So goodnight lad, goodnight love,
We have a long day ahead of us tomorrow,
But it will be perfect all the same,
Goodnight, goodnight son.

Acknowledgements

A big thank you to everyone who has helped me in my career so far. A massive thank you to Joelle Taylor for her thorough guidance. A big thank you to Pete Hunter and Apples and Snakes for their generous funding. Thank you to Michael and Rosy from Hammer & Tongue, Emily from BBC 1Xtra, Liz, Laurie and Yomi from Words First, Grant and Craig from Cling Film TV and all the guys at Lemonade Money.

Thank you to everyone who has invited me to perform at their poetry nights and festivals and everyone who has hired me to teach. Thank you to LAW Magazine, Louise from the Pebble Trust, David Judd from the V&A, Chima and Belinda from Born::Free Fridays, James from SPAEKING, everyone at STEEZ, Tom Hines and the legendary Herbie Flowers. Thank you to Stamp the Wax and Tom Charles Sayer for their reviews. Thank you to Spit the Atom for their constant support. Thank you to Zak, Tezz and Amyn amongst all my friends. Thank you to Pollie for coming to watch half my performances this year. Thank you to Normanton Street, Rob and Josh for putting music to my words. Thank you to everyone who has academically inspired me from Mr Taljaard at Varndean School to my lecturers at Goldsmiths University. Thank you to Adam and everyone at AudioActive, the Crew Club and the Brighton Youth Centre for believing in me when I was finding my feet as a performer of words. There are many more people I would like to acknowledge but unfortunately I do not have space to name everyone.

Thank you to my grandmas, to my aunty and foremost to my mum, without whom I would be nowhere.

Lightning Source UK Ltd.
Milton Keynes UK
UKOW06f0308080616

275797UK00007B/153/P